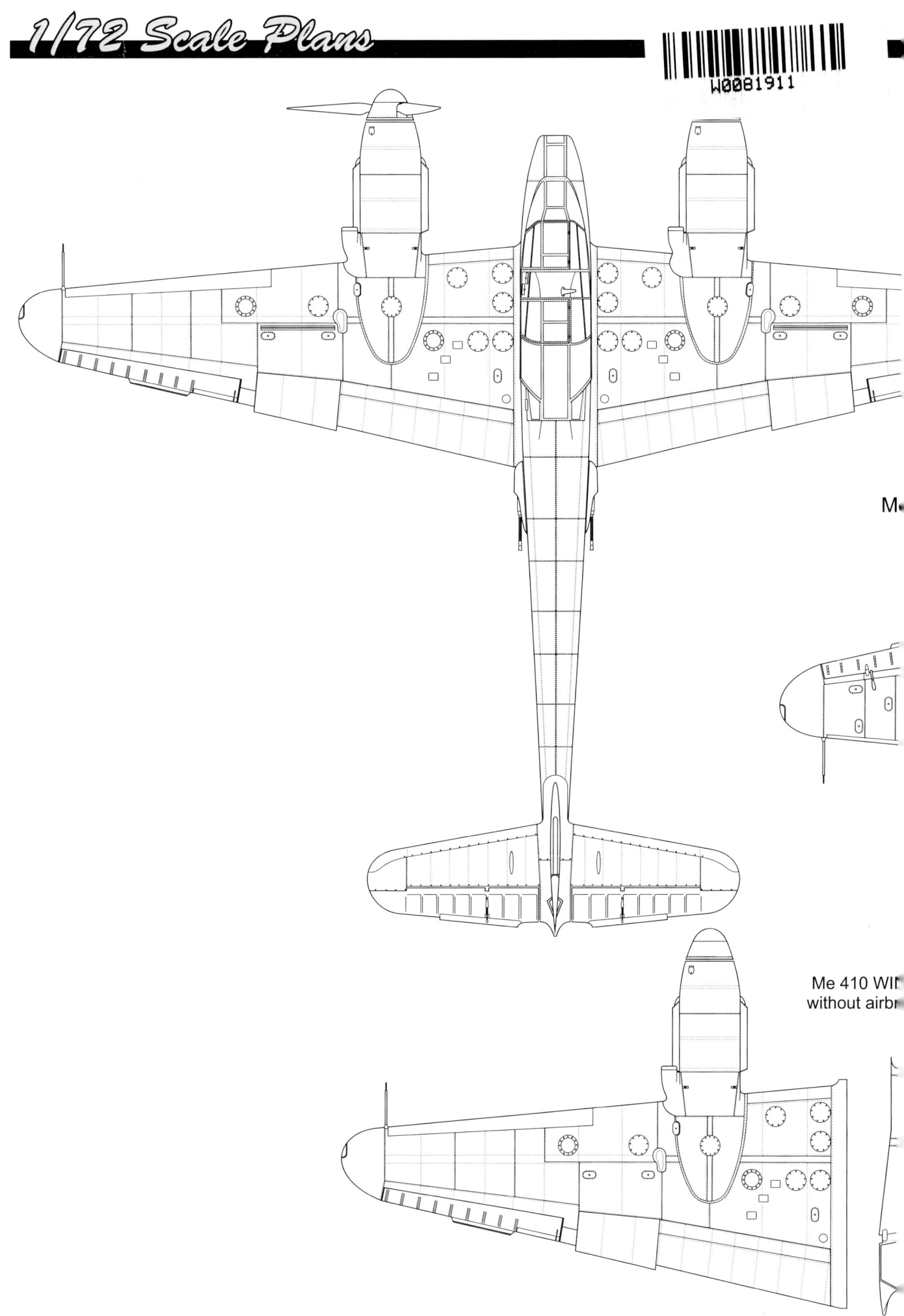

M

Me 410 WI
without airb

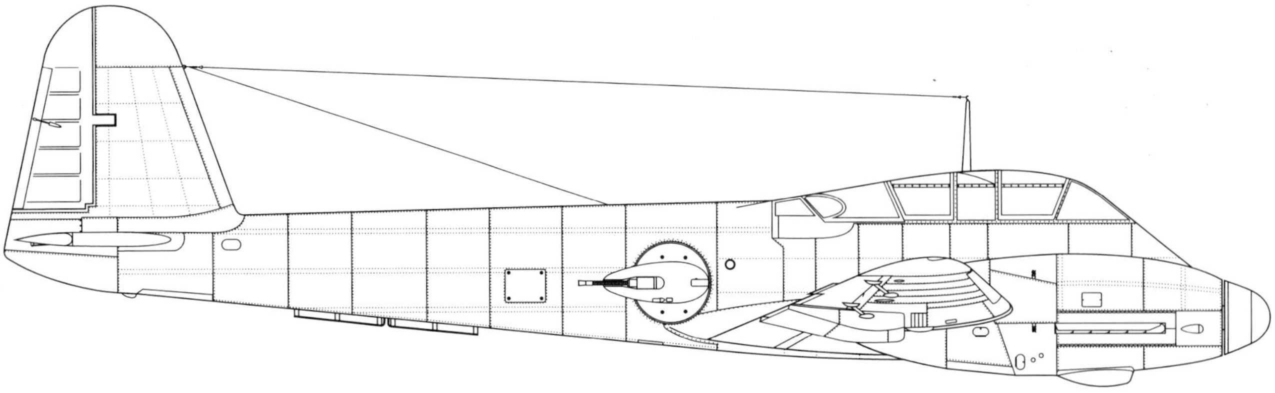

A-1

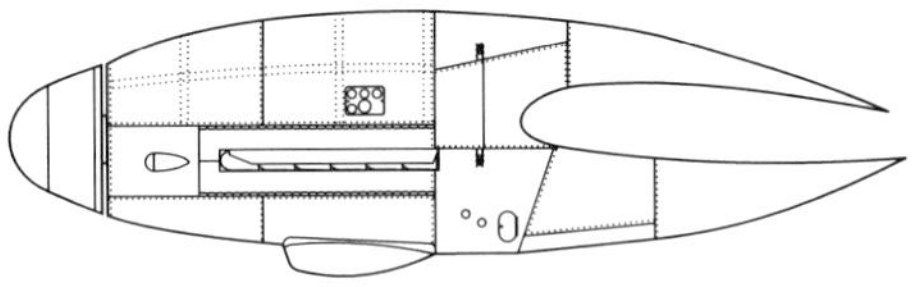

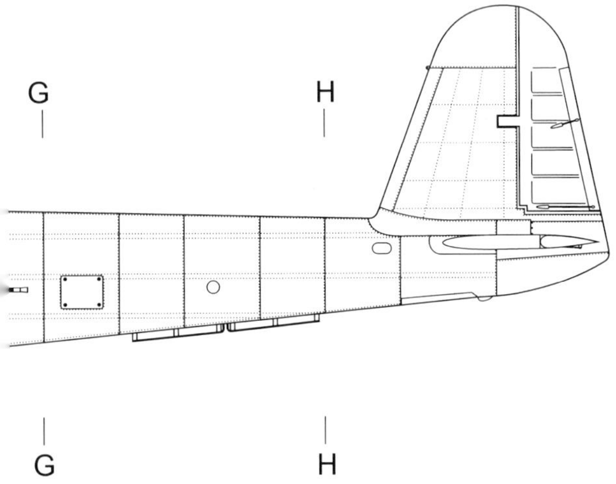

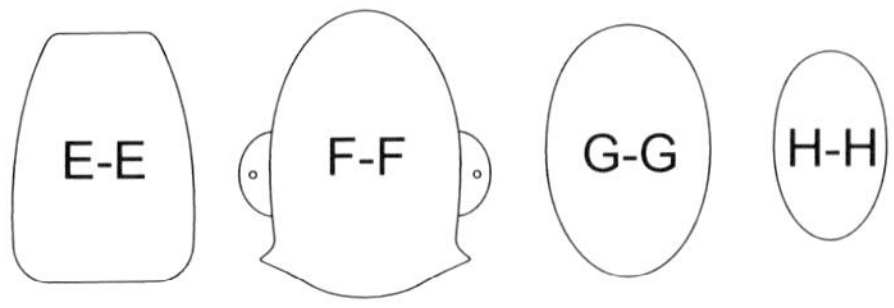

G

H

E-E

F-F

G-G

H-H

G

H

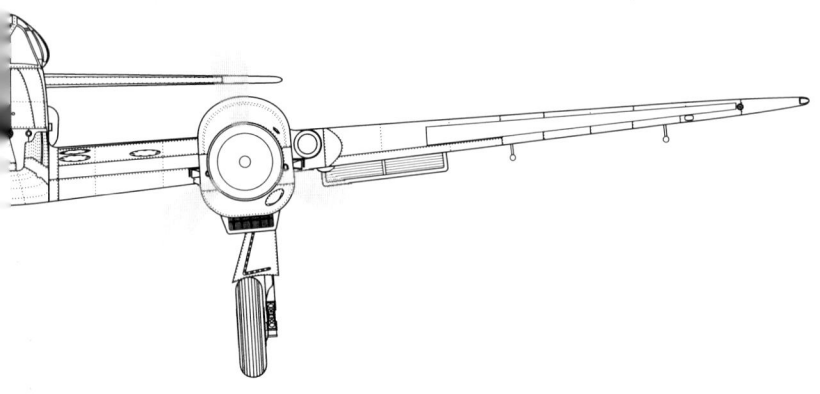

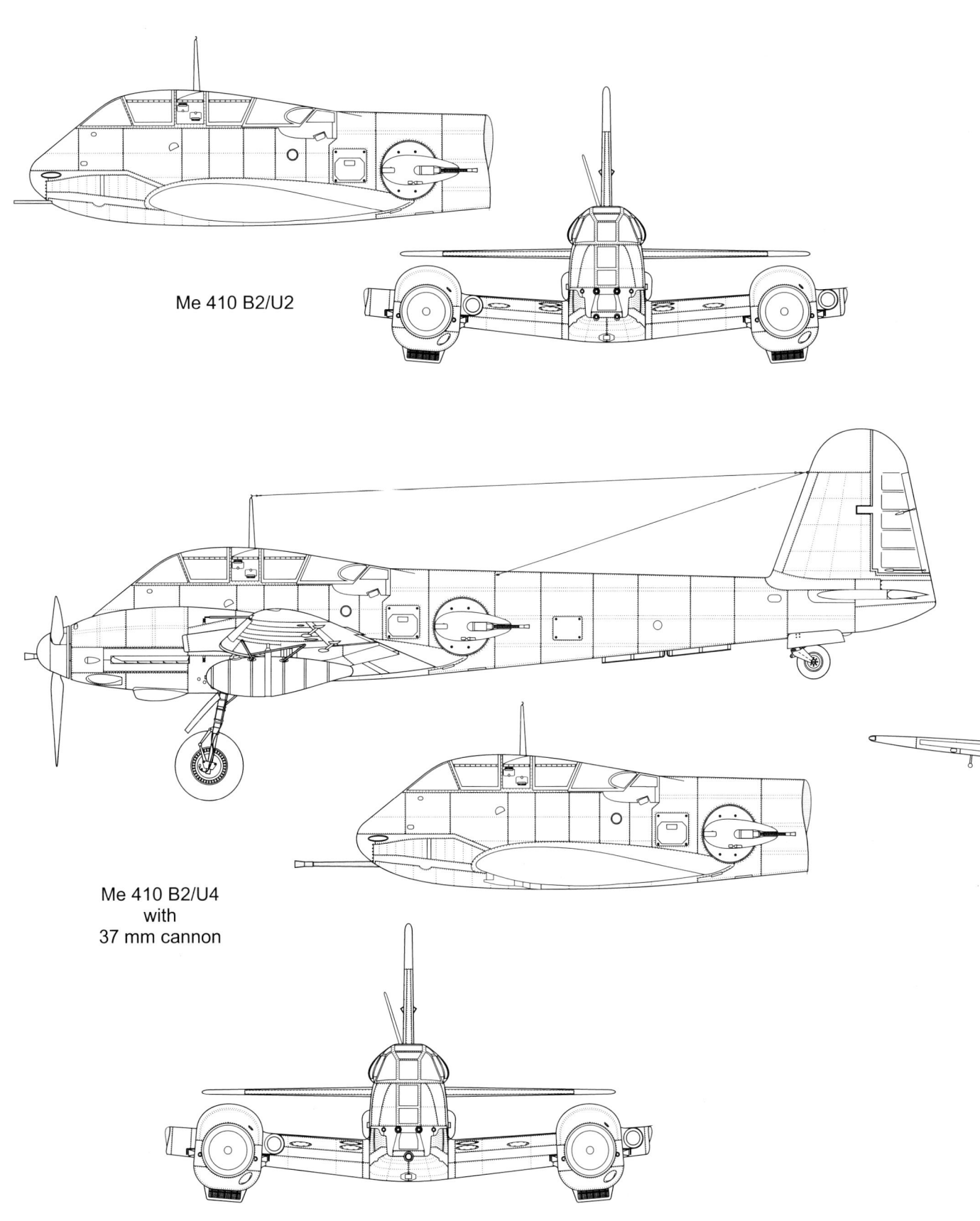

Me 410 B2/U2

Me 410 B2/U4
with
37 mm cannon

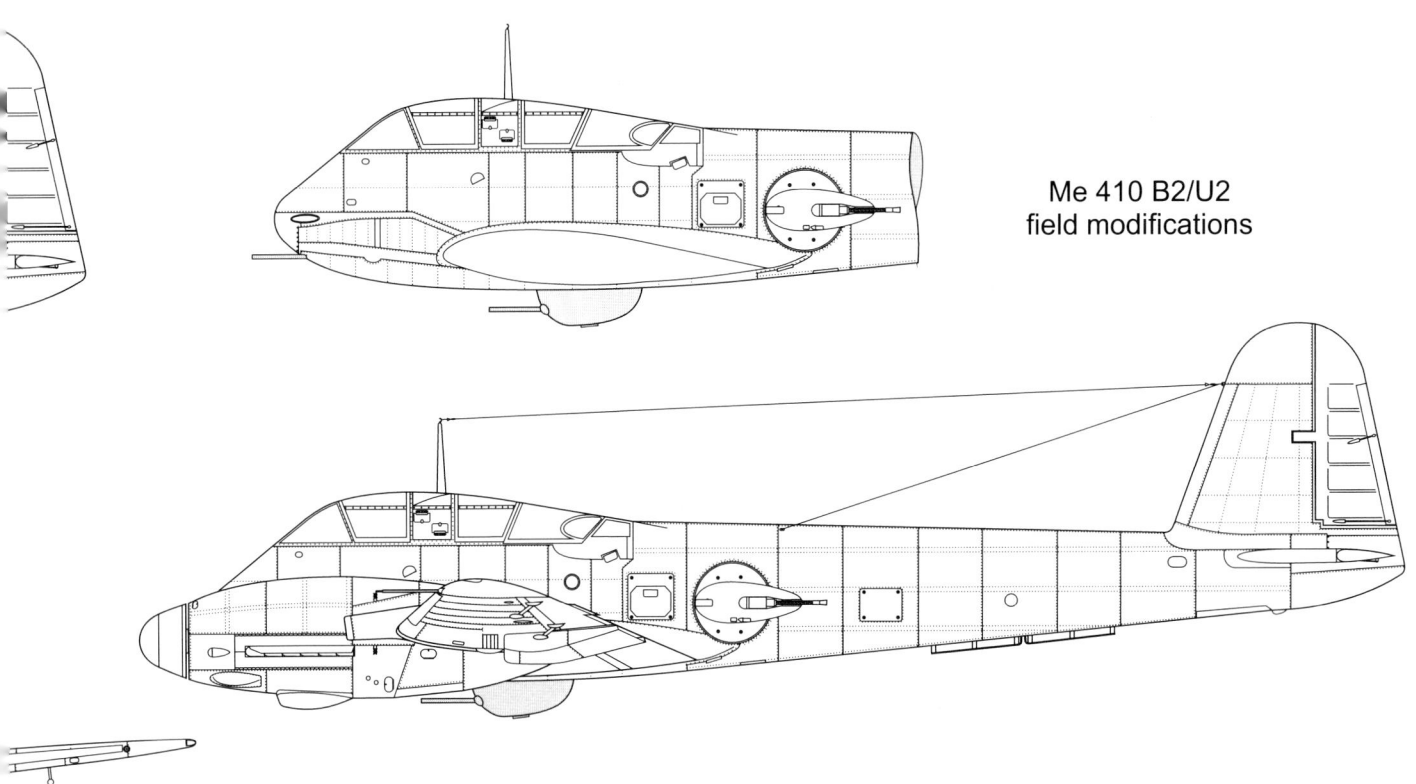

Me 410 B2/U2
field modifications

Me 410 B1/U2

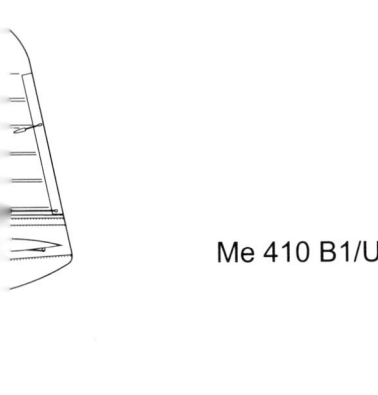

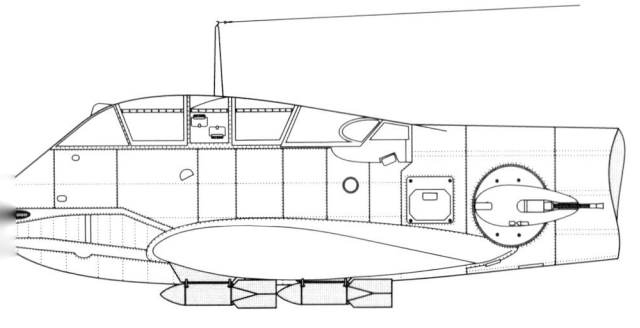

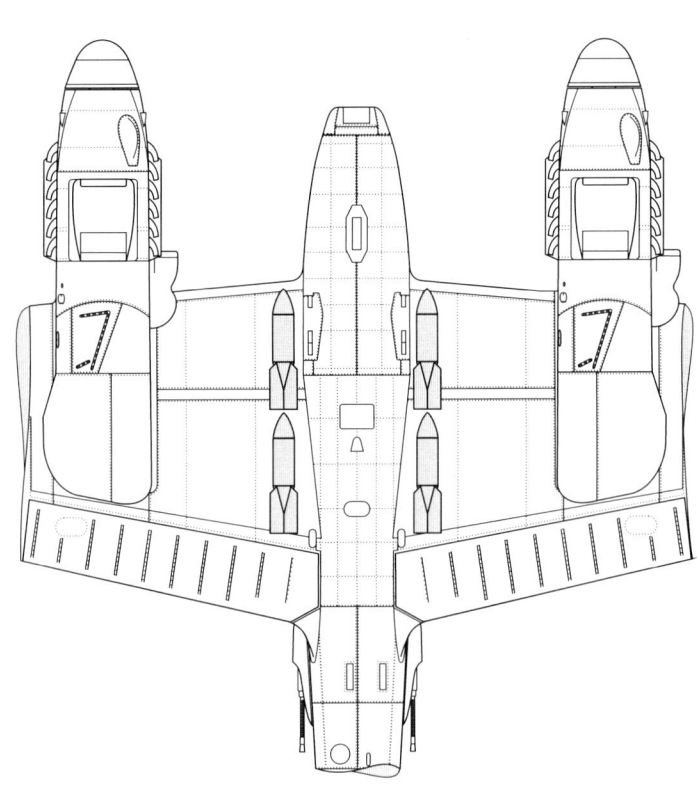

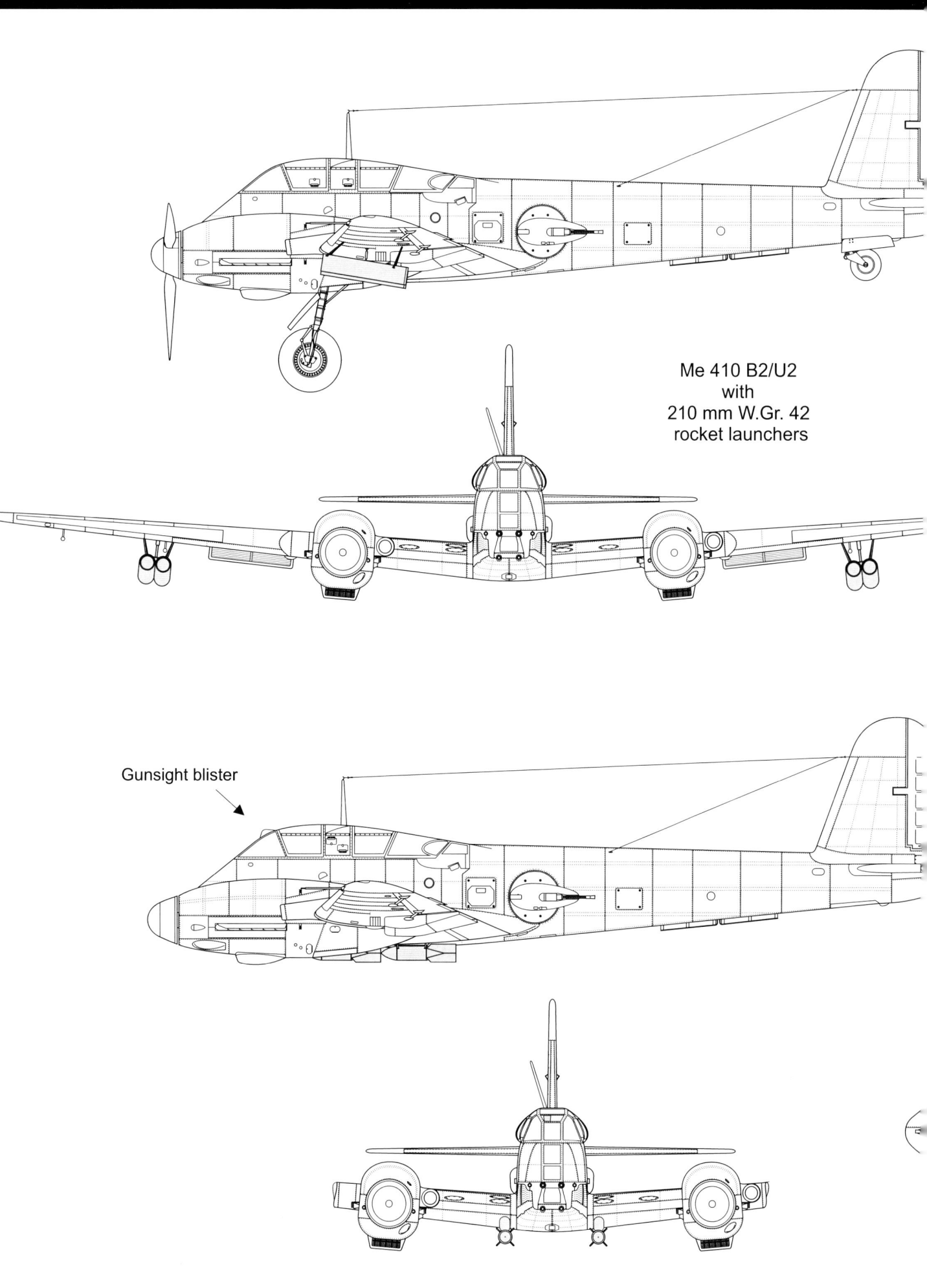

Me 410 B2/U2
with
210 mm W.Gr. 42
rocket launchers

Gunsight blister

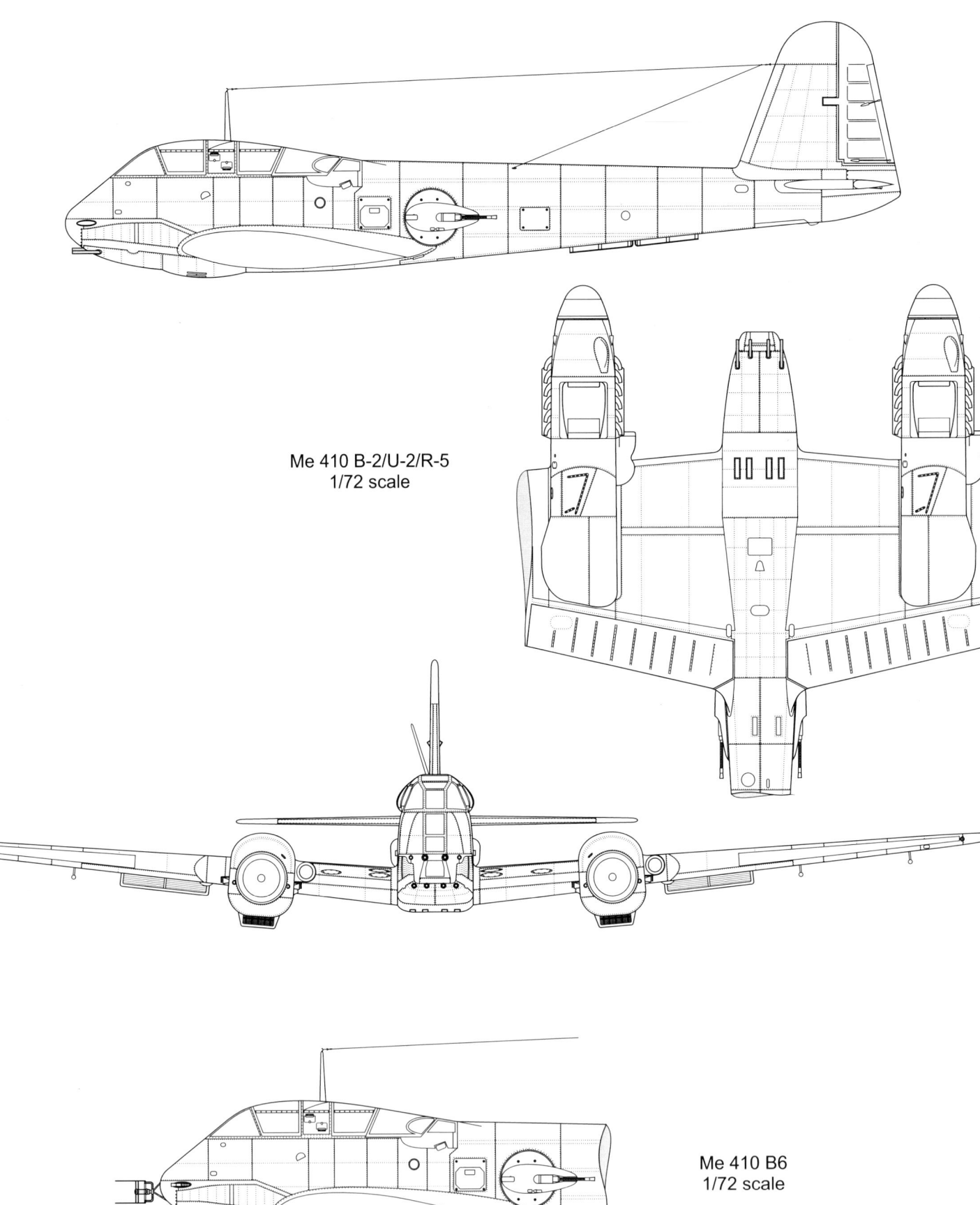

Me 410 B-2/U-2/R-5
1/72 scale

Me 410 B6
1/72 scale

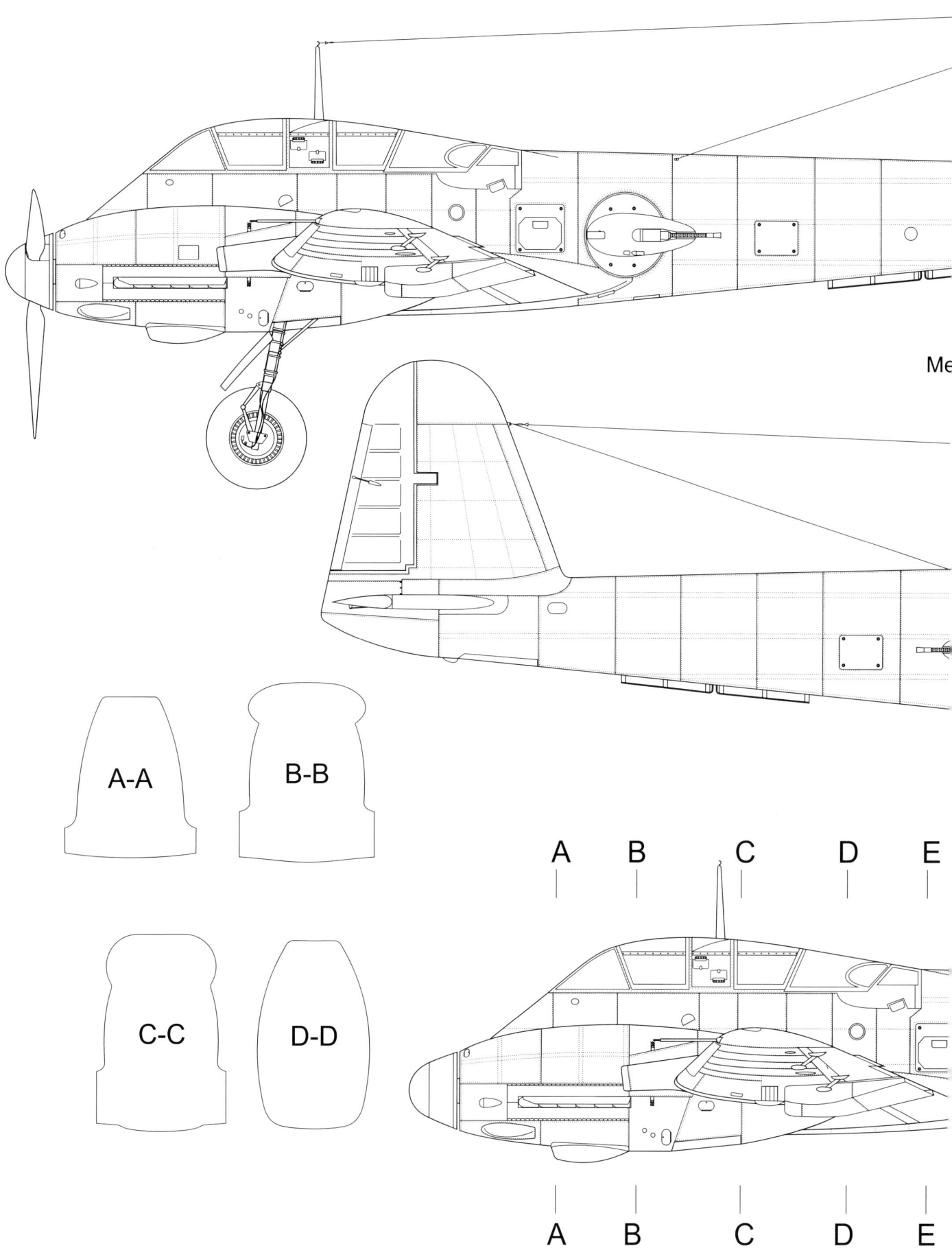

Me

A-A   B-B

C-C   D-D

A   B   C   D   E

A   B   C   D   E

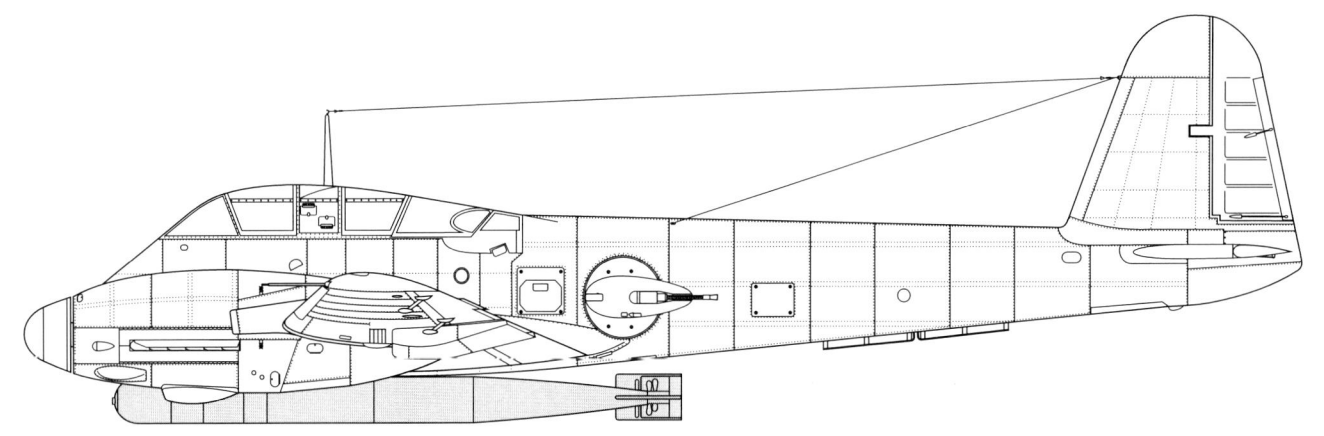

Me 410 B-5
with LT 950 torpedo

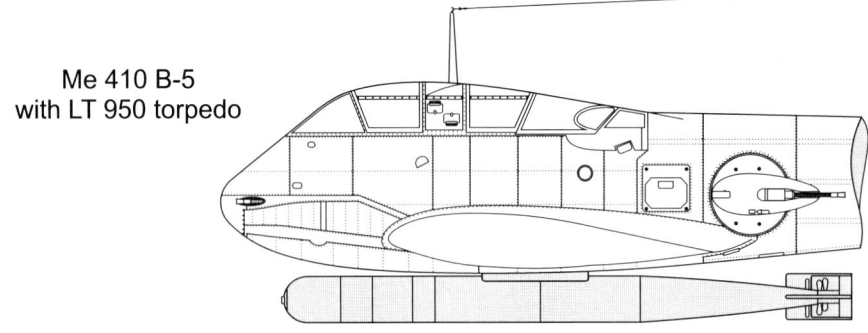

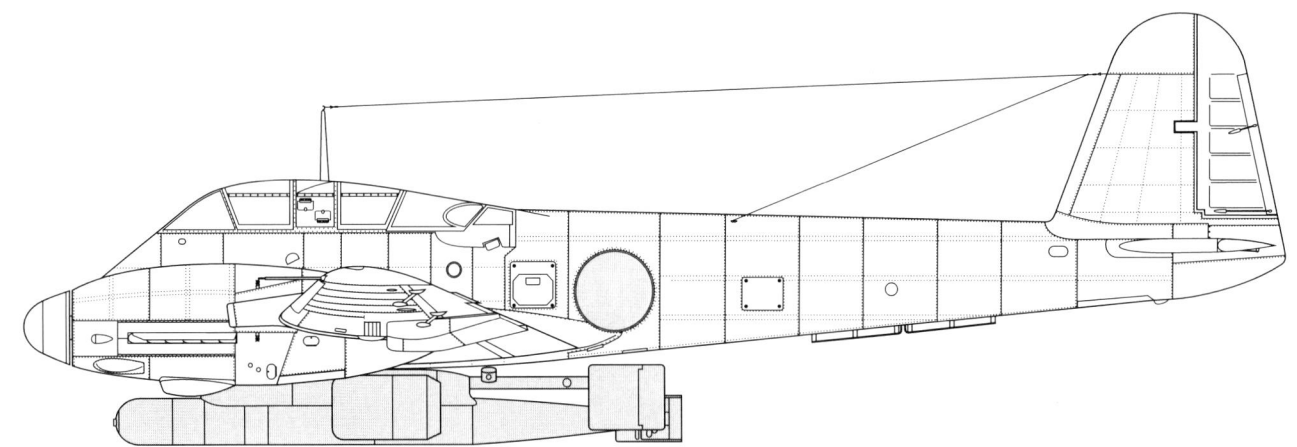

Me 410 B-5
with LT 950 / L-10 torpedo
and reduced
defensive armament

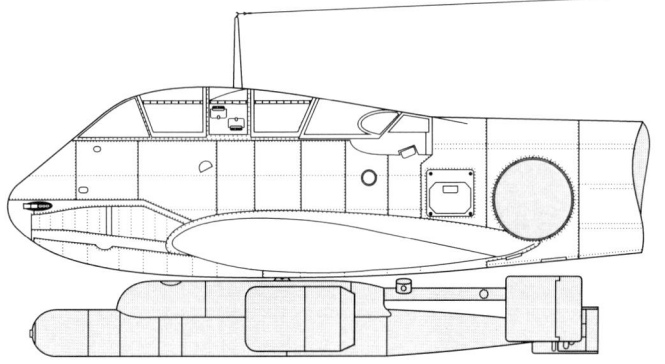

© Dariusz Karnas
MMP GRAPHICS

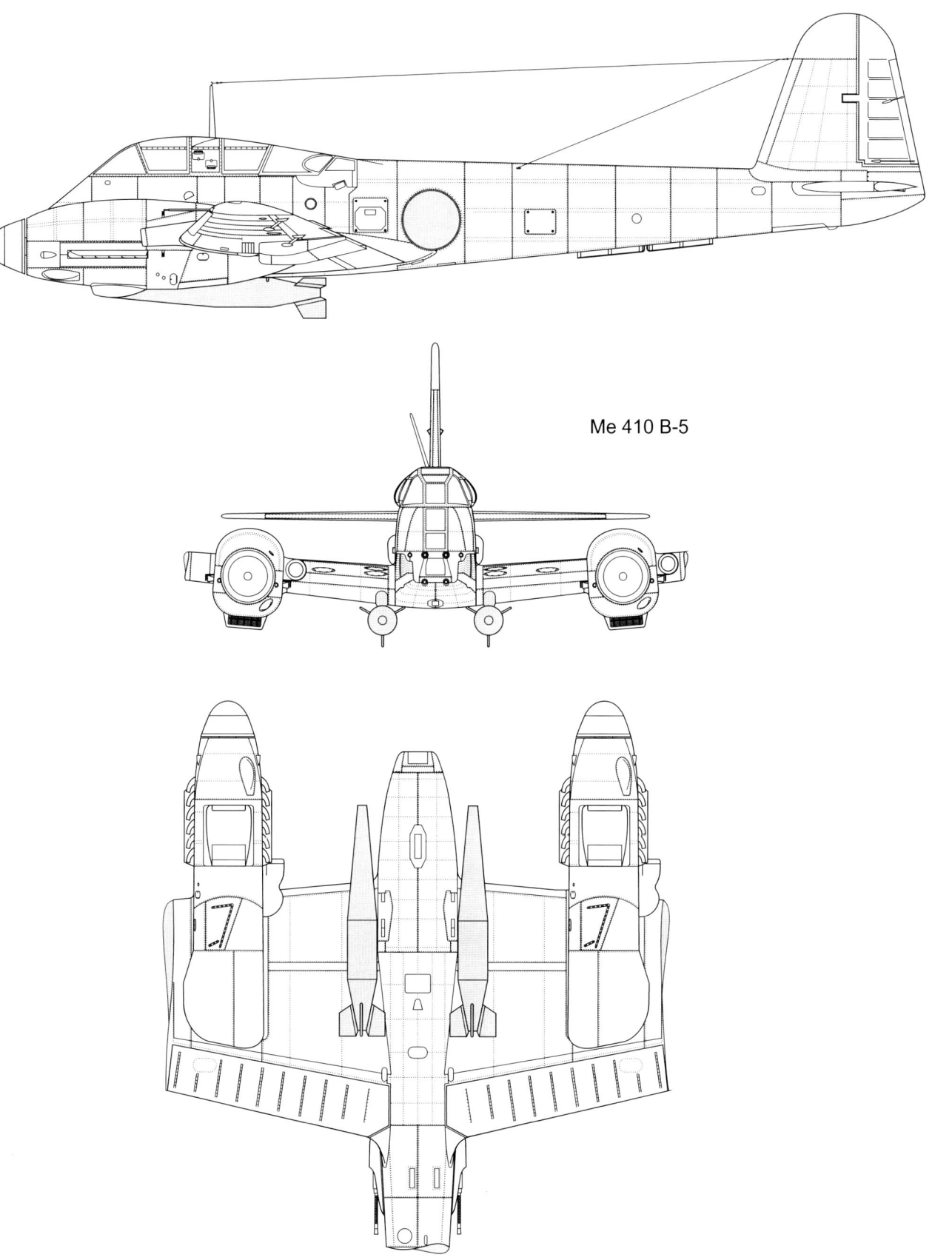

Me 410 B-5

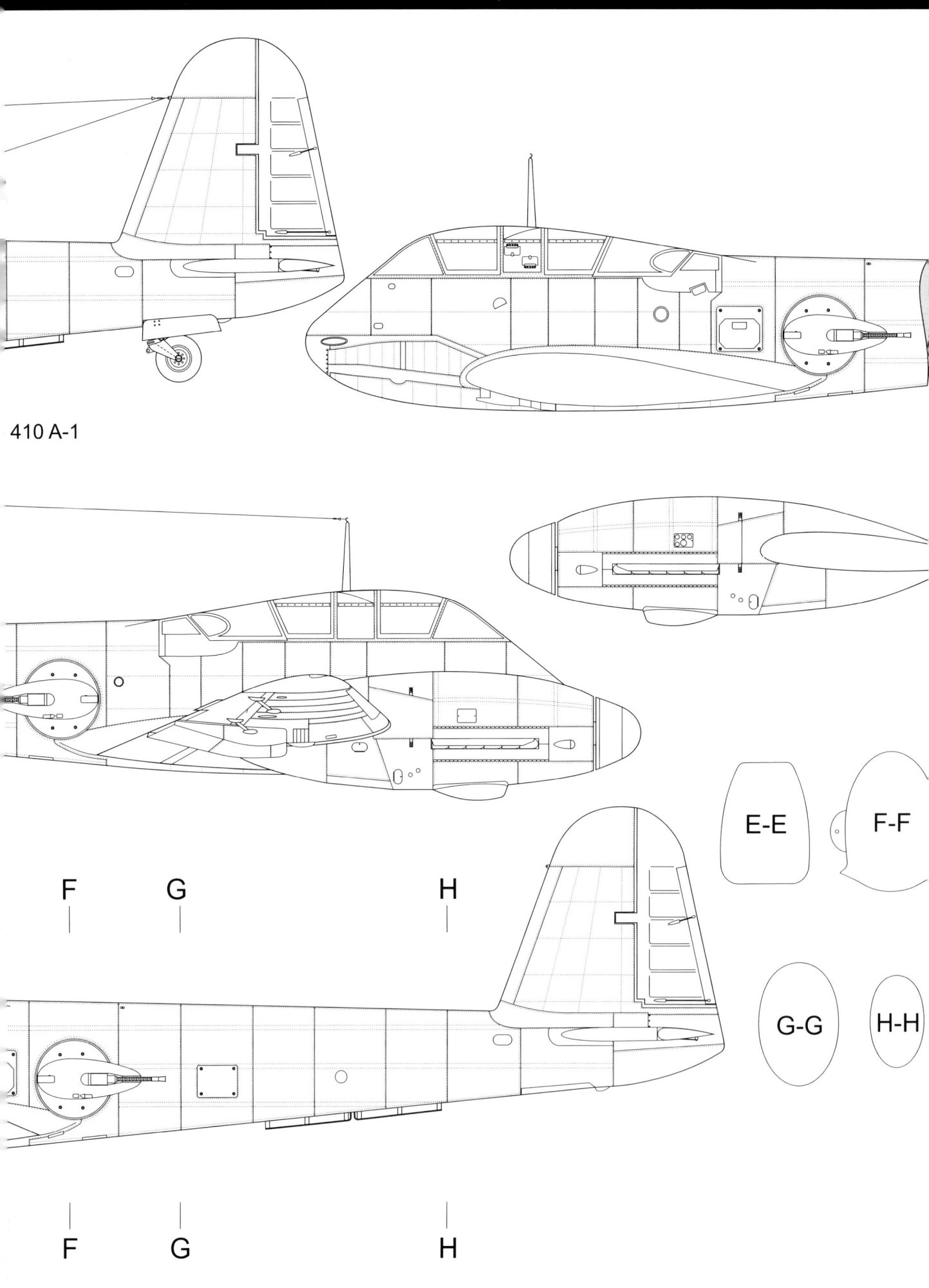

410 A-1

F   G   H

E-E   F-F

G-G   H-H

F   G   H

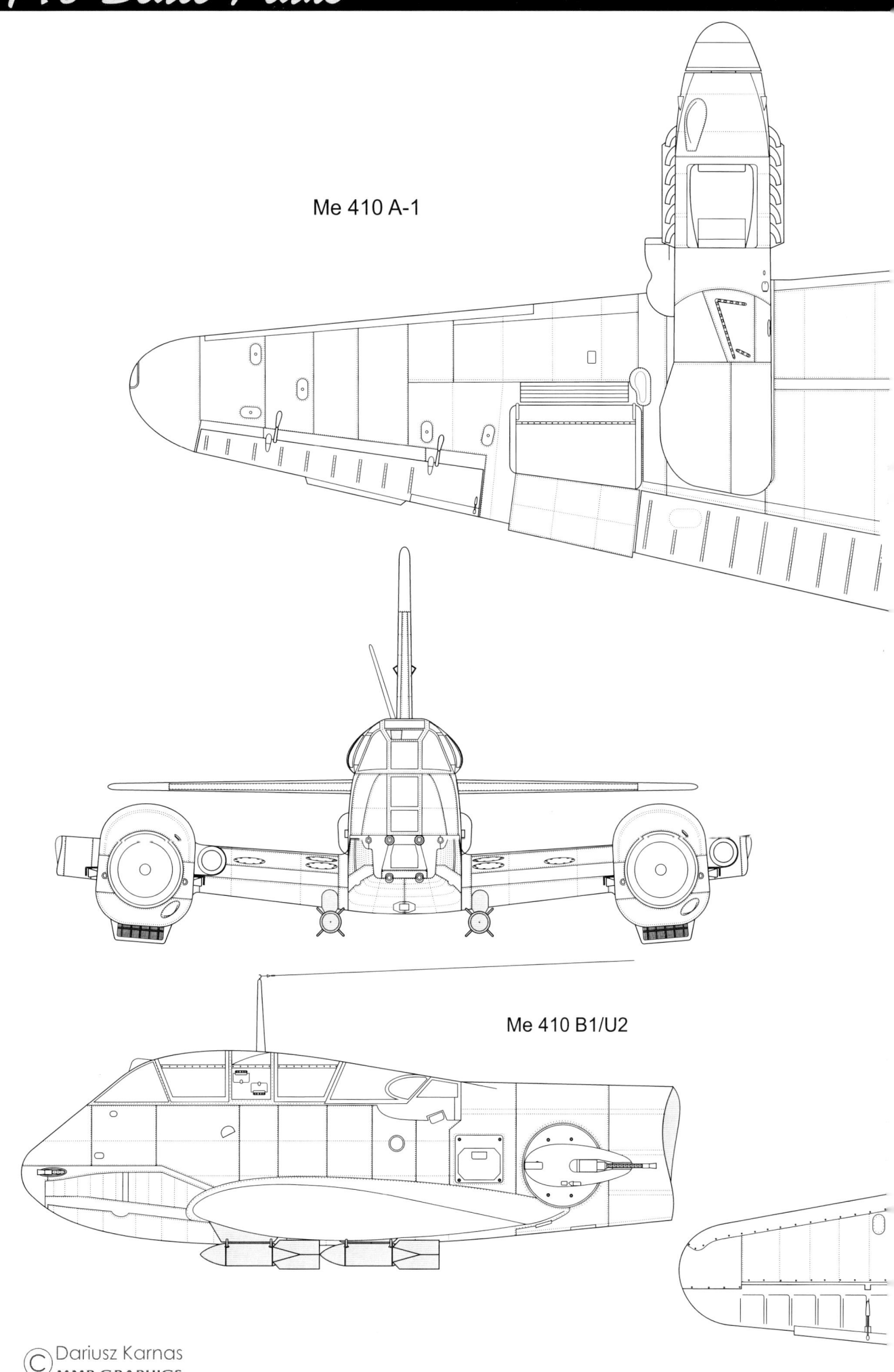

Me 410 A-1

Me 410 B1/U2

Me 410 WINGS
without airbrakes

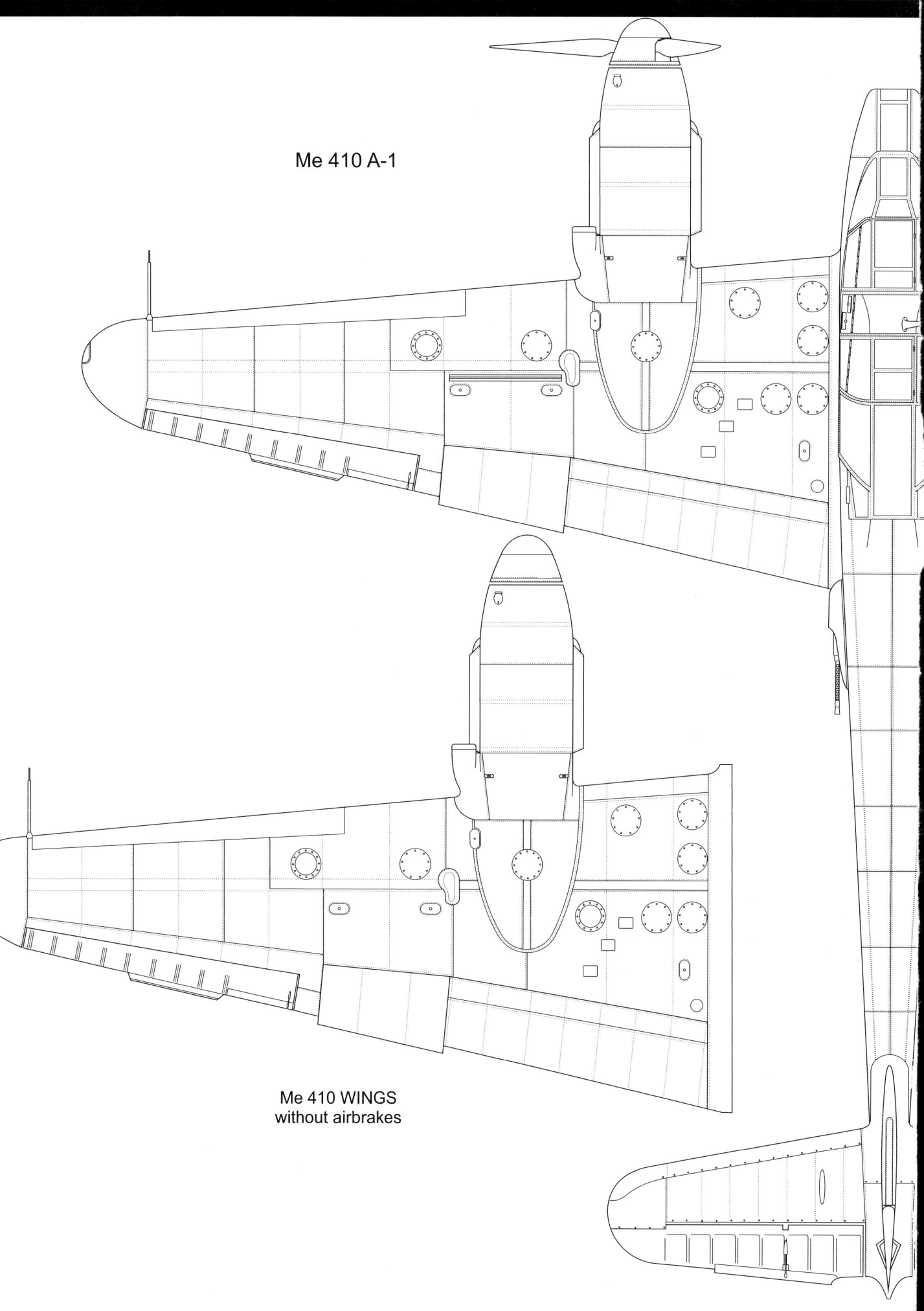

Me 410 A-1

Me 410 WINGS
without airbrakes

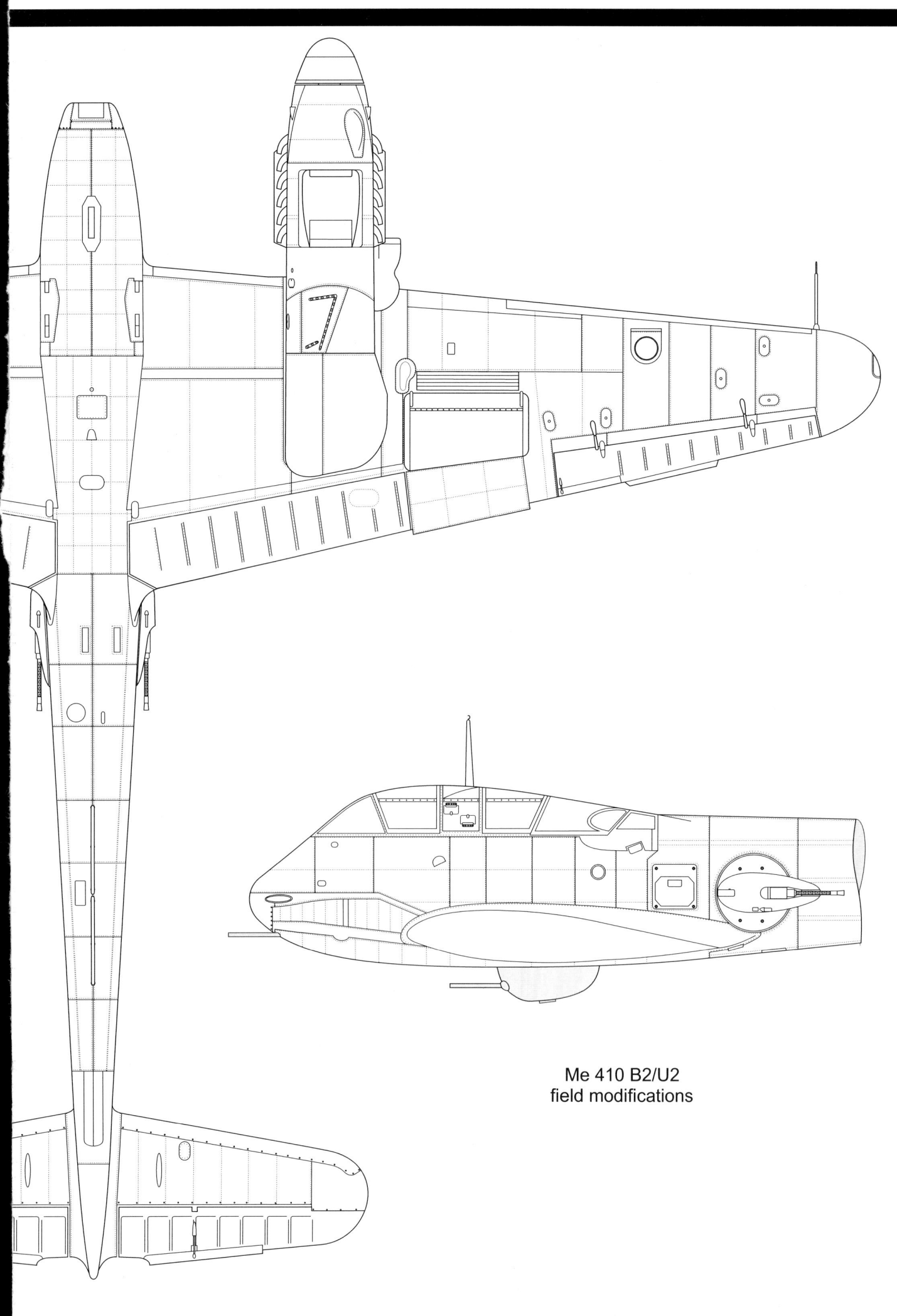

Me 410 B2/U2
field modifications

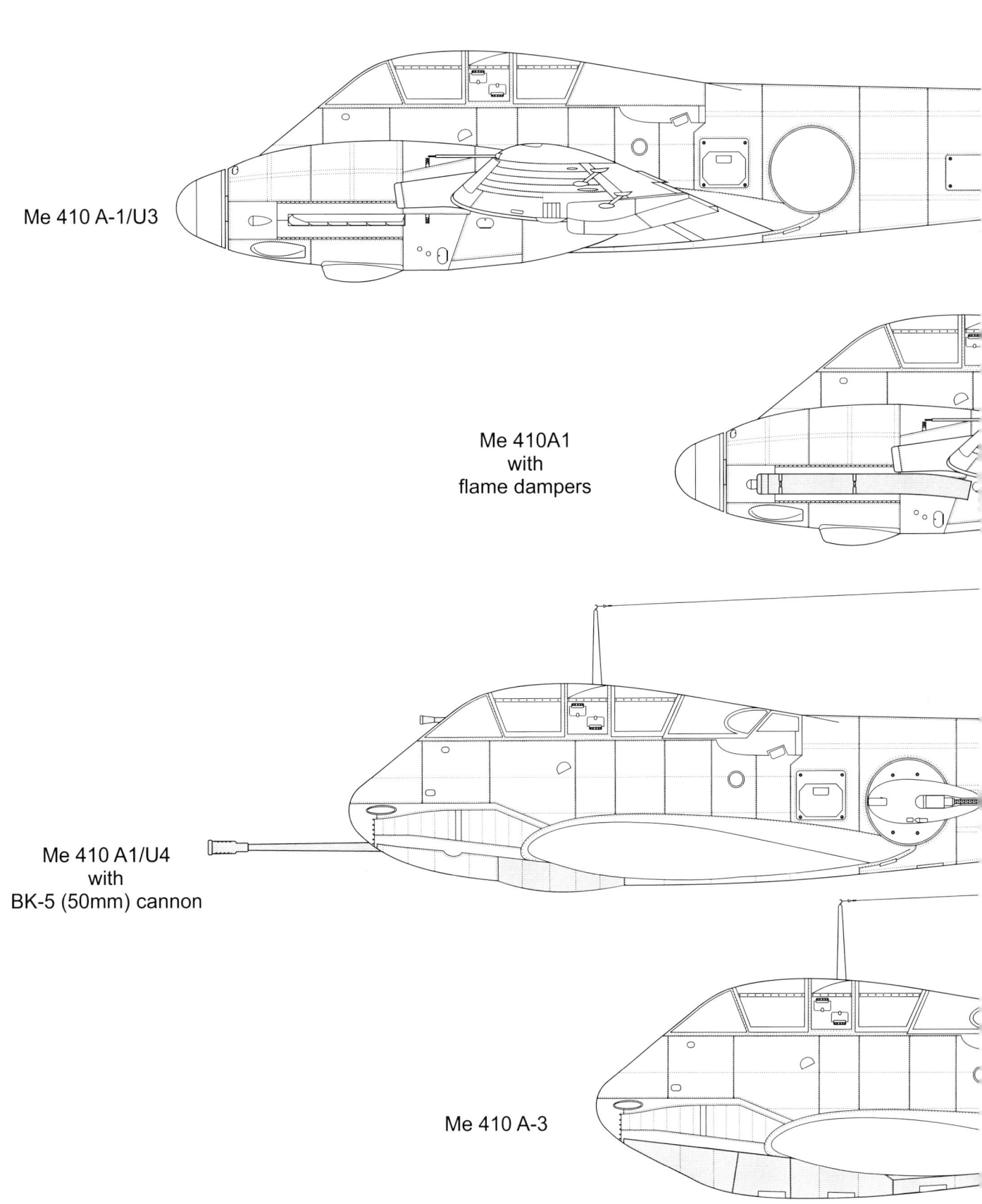

Me 410 A-1/U3

Me 410A1
with
flame dampers

Me 410 A1/U4
with
BK-5 (50mm) cannon

Me 410 A-3

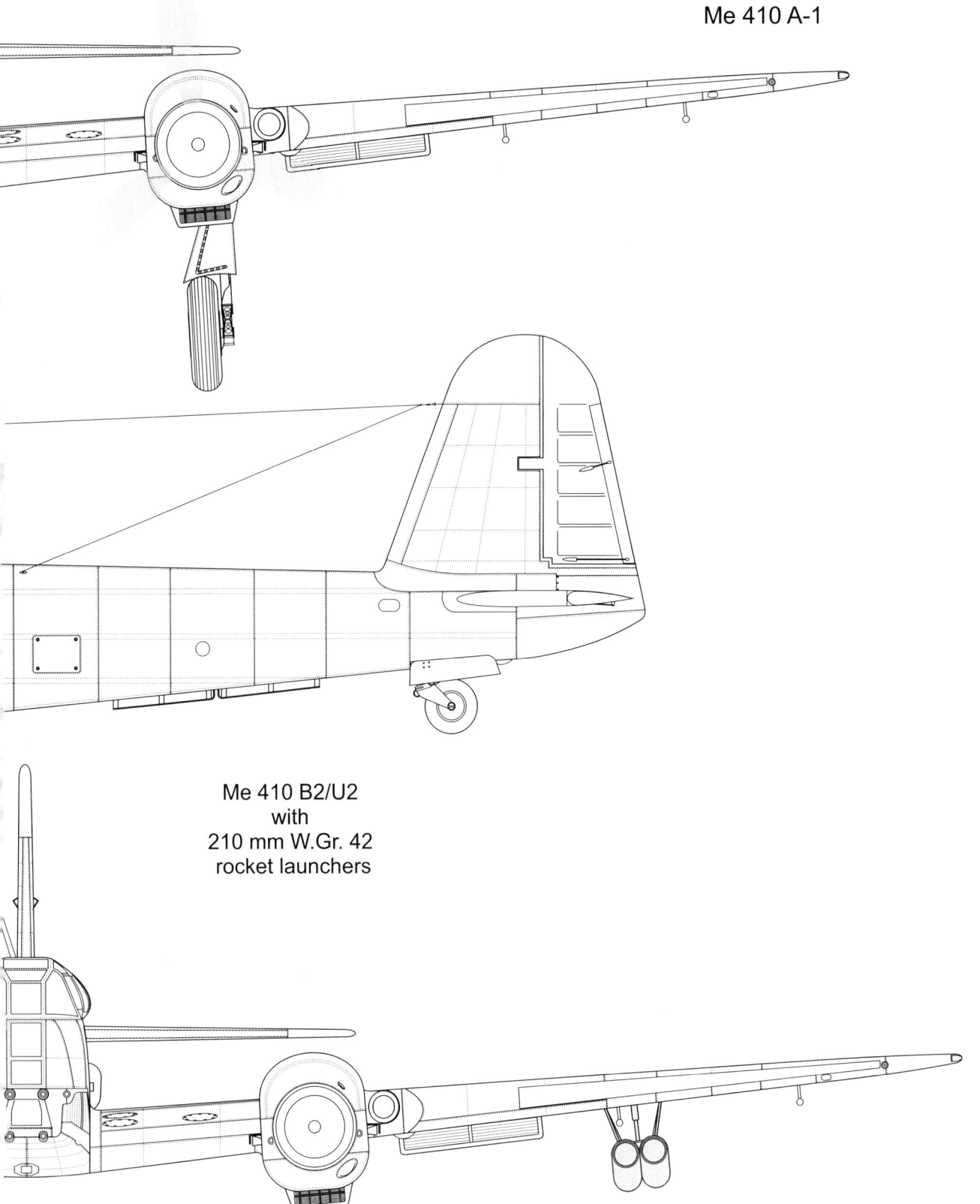

Me 410 A-1

Me 410 B2/U2
with
210 mm W.Gr. 42
rocket launchers

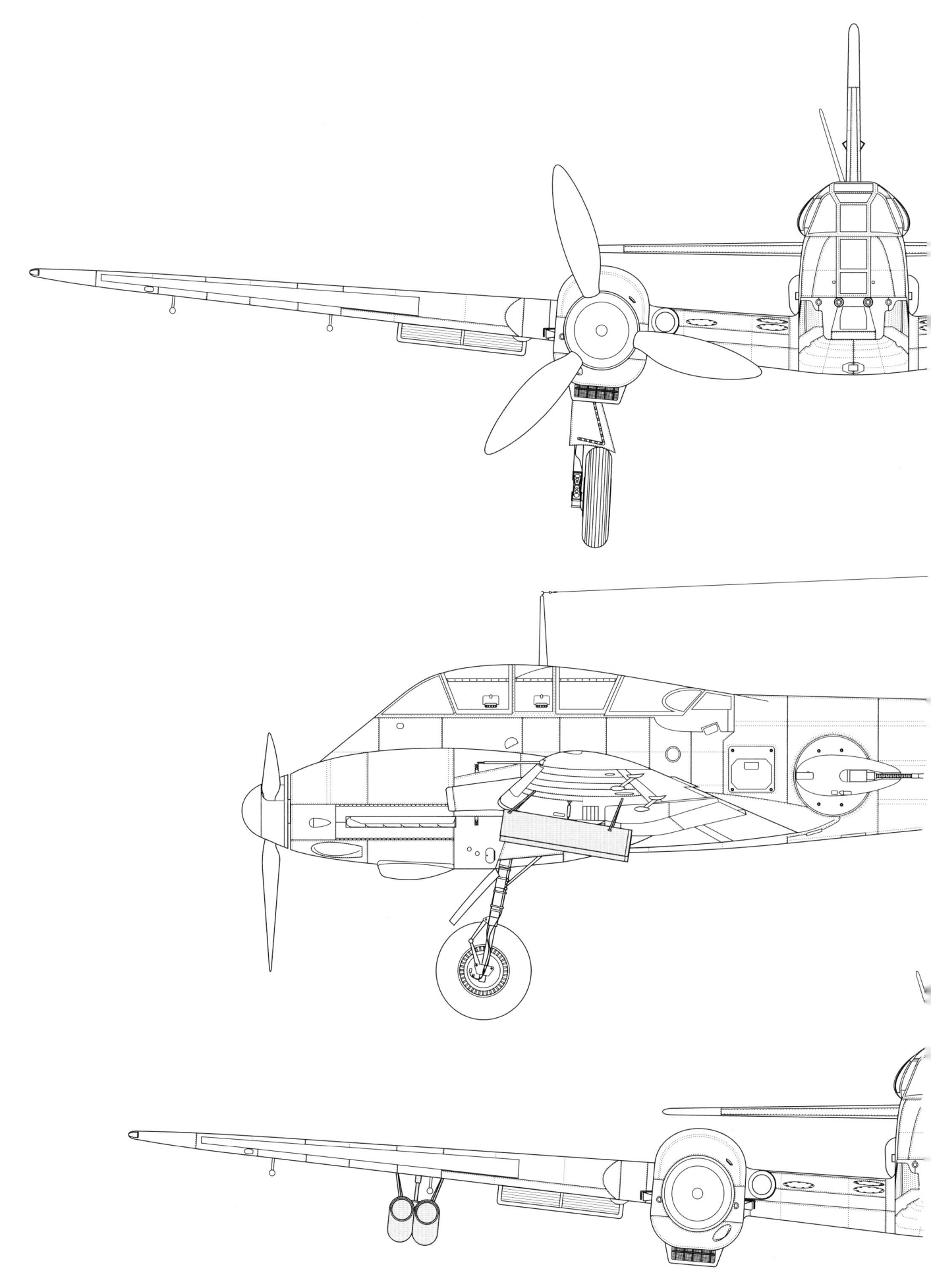